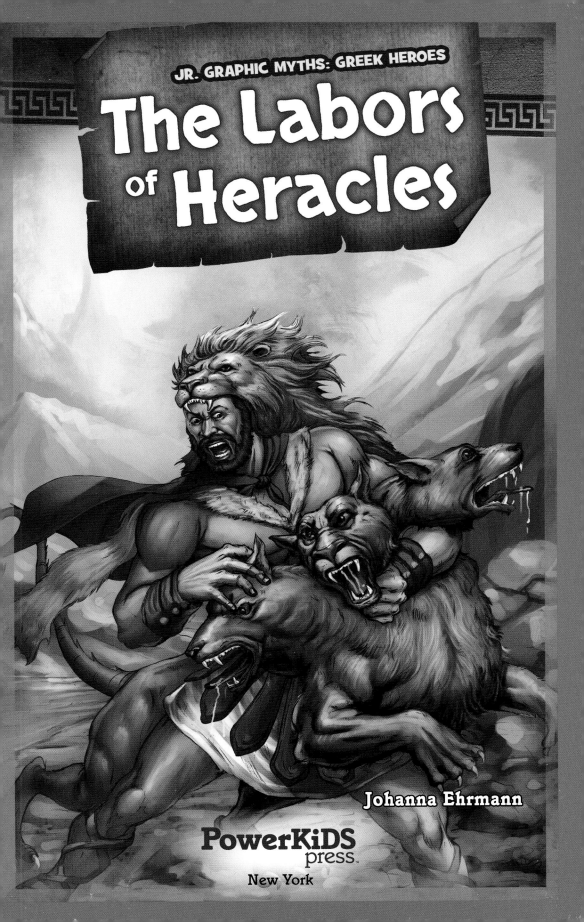

JR. GRAPHIC MYTHS: GREEK HEROES

The Labors of Heracles

Johanna Ehrmann

PowerKiDS press

New York

Published in 2014 by The Rosen Publishing Group, Inc.
29 East 21st Street, New York, NY 10010

First Edition

Editor: Joanne Randolph
Book Design: Contentra Technologies
Illustrations: Contentra Technologies

Publisher's Cataloging Data

Ehrmann, Johanna.
The labors of Heracles / by Johanna Ehrmann. — First Edition.

p. cm. — (Jr. graphic myths: Greek heroes)
Includes index.
ISBN 978-1-4777-6224-0 (library binding) — ISBN 978-1-4777-6225-7 (pbk.) —
ISBN 978-1-4777-6226-4 (6-pack)
1. Hercules (Roman mythology) — Juvenile literature. I. Ehrmann, Johanna. II. Title.
BL820.H5. E37 2014
398.2—d23

Manufactured in the United States of America
CPSIA Compliance Information: Batch #W14PK1: For Further Information contact Rosen Publishing, New York, New York at 1-800-237-9932

Contents

Introduction

Heracles was perhaps the greatest hero in all of Greek **mythology**. His father was Zeus, the king of the gods. Zeus fell in love with Alcmene, a **mortal** woman. They had a child named Heracles. The boy was raised by Alcmene and her husband, Amphitryon. This made Hera, the goddess of women and marriage, and Zeus's wife, very angry. She directed her fury at Heracles, who grew up to be an immensely strong and brave man.

Main Characters

 Heracles Called Hercules in Roman mythology. One of ancient Greece's greatest mythological heroes.

 Eurystheus Cousin of Heracles and king of Tiryns in Mycenae. It is located on the Peloponnesian Peninsula.

 Hera Wife of Zeus, queen of the gods.

 Iolaus Nephew and faithful servant of Heracles.

 Augeas King of Elis.

Hippolyta Queen of the **Amazons**.

The Labors of Heracles

ONE NIGHT WHEN THEY WERE YOUNG, HERACLES AND HIS BROTHER IPHICLES WERE ASLEEP. HERA SENT TWO SERPENTS TO KILL HERACLES. INSTEAD, HERACLES PICKED UP THE SERPENTS AND BROKE THEIR NECKS.

DID YOU SEE THAT?

HE'S AN UNUSUAL BABY.

AS HERACLES GREW, HE BECAME STRONGER AND STRONGER. WHEN HE WAS ANGRY, HE SOMETIMES FORGOT HOW STRONG HE WAS. ONCE, HE KILLED HIS MUSIC TEACHER BY MISTAKE.

AS A RESULT, AMPHITRYON, ALCMENE'S HUSBAND, SENT HERACLES AWAY TO A FARM IN THE COUNTRY.

IT IS FOR YOUR OWN GOOD.

I'M SORRY, FATHER. I DIDN'T MEAN TO DO IT.

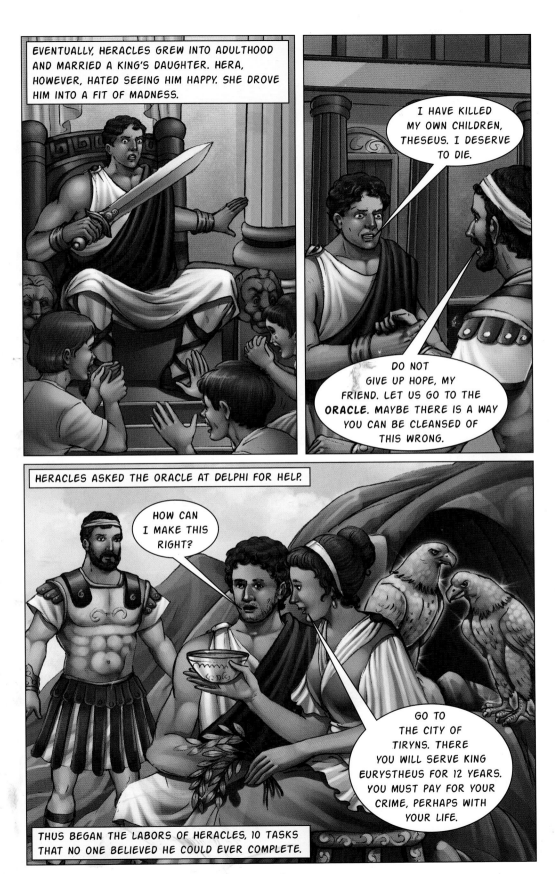

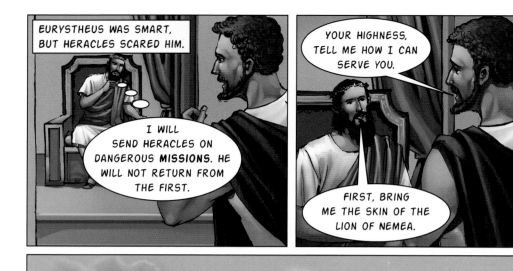

EURYSTHEUS WAS SMART, BUT HERACLES SCARED HIM.

I WILL SEND HERACLES ON DANGEROUS **MISSIONS**. HE WILL NOT RETURN FROM THE FIRST.

YOUR HIGHNESS, TELL ME HOW I CAN SERVE YOU.

FIRST, BRING ME THE SKIN OF THE LION OF NEMEA.

THE LION WAS FIERCE AND HAD CAUSED GREAT **DESTRUCTION**. ARROWS BOUNCED OFF IT. THE LION JUST SHOOK ITS HEAD WHEN HERACLES CLUBBED IT. FINALLY, HERACLES USED HIS BARE HANDS TO STRANGLE THE BEAST.

HERACLES SKINNED THE LION. THEN HE RETURNED TO THE PALACE, WEARING THE LION'S **PELT**.

YOUR HIGHNESS, WHAT SHALL I DO NEXT?

DON'T COME HERE AGAIN. WAIT OUTSIDE THE CITY AND I WILL SEND A **HERALD**.

8

NEXT, EURYSTHEUS SENT HERACLES TO CRETE FOR ANOTHER IMPOSSIBLE TASK, TO CAPTURE A WILD BULL.

IF THIS WIND HOLDS UP, WE WILL MAKE LANDFALL BY EVENING.

THAT'S GOOD. I NEED SOME EXERCISE.

Greece

Athens

Mycenae

Crete

THERE'S CRETE!

ANY SIGN OF THE BULL?

THIS GUY IS STRONG, BUT I AM STRONGER.

I'VE GOT YOU NOW.

THIS BULL WAS STRONG AND SAID TO BREATHE FLAMES. IT WAS THE FATHER OF THE MINOTAUR, AND IT WAS SACRED TO THE SEA GOD, POSEIDON.

HERACLES BROUGHT THE BULL BACK TO EURYSTHEUS AND WAITED OUTSIDE THE CITY WHILE THE KING SPOKE TO HERA.

THIS WAS NOT AS HARD AS I THOUGHT. THE KING WILL BE PLEASED.

ALLOW ME TO SACRIFICE THIS BULL IN YOUR HONOR.

THE IDEA **OFFENDS ME!** HERACLES'S DEEDS DO NOT DESERVE TO BE HONORED. RELEASE THE BULL.

DIOMEDES, A CHIEF IN THRACE, HAD FOUR HORSES SO WILD THAT THEY ATE HUMAN FLESH. HE WAS A CRUEL MAN AND VERY UNKIND TO STRANGERS. HERACLES KILLED DIOMEDES, CAPTURED THE HORSES, AND BROUGHT THEM BACK TO EURYSTHEUS.

A THREE-BODIED CREATURE NAMED GERYON HAD RED CATTLE ON THE NORTH COAST OF AFRICA. SOME SAY THAT ON THE WAY TO AFRICA, HERACLES SPLIT A LARGE MOUNTAIN IN TWO, MAKING AN ENTRANCE INTO THE MEDITERRANEAN SEA.

PUSHING THIS MOUNTAIN APART IS HARDER THAN I THOUGHT IT WOULD BE.

HERACLES HAD TO KILL A GUARD DOG, SOME **SENTINELS**, AND GERYON BEFORE HE GOT THE CATTLE. HERA MADE THE DIFFICULT TRIP HOME TOUGHER.

THESE BITING FLIES WILL SLOW YOU DOWN.

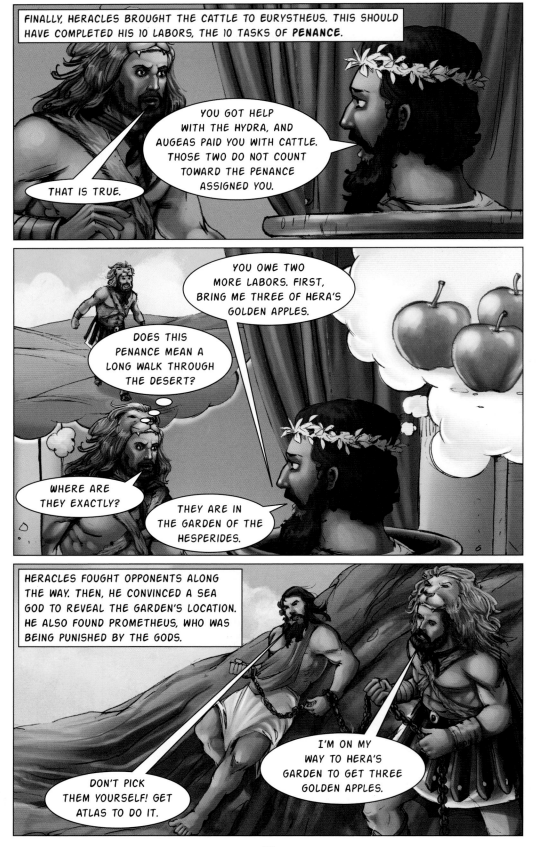

Historical Background and Map

Hera and Heracles

Heracles had a powerful enemy in the goddess Hera. At birth, he was given the name Alcides. Alcmene and Amphitryon changed his name to Heracles, meaning "glory of Hera." They were probably trying to find a way to please the goddess. Unfortunately, this does not seem to have worked. It was the oracle who told Heracles to serve his cousin. However, ancient writers Euripides, Ovid, and Virgil all agree that Hera was the driving force behind Heracles's labors.

In some accounts, Hera meddled even more in Heracles's life. It is said that she delayed Heracles's birth. She wanted his cousin to be born first and rule in his place. Others suggest that Hera sent a giant crab to nip Heracles's foot while he was battling the Hydra. Clearly, she wanted to make these tasks impossible. Ironically, Hera's opposition may be the reason for Heracles's fame and great triumphs. Had she not challenged him, he might not have achieved nearly as much.

The Labors of Heracles

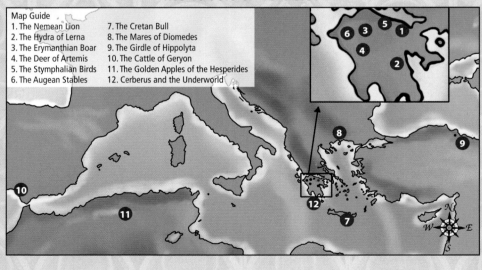

Map Guide
1. The Nemean Lion
2. The Hydra of Lerna
3. The Erymanthian Boar
4. The Deer of Artemis
5. The Stymphalian Birds
6. The Augean Stables
7. The Cretan Bull
8. The Mares of Diomedes
9. The Girdle of Hippolyta
10. The Cattle of Geryon
11. The Golden Apples of the Hesperides
12. Cerberus and the Underworld

Glossary

Amazons (A-muh-zonz) Fierce female warriors who, according to legend, lived in Scythia.

boar (BOR) A wild male pig.

destruction (dih-STRUK-shun) Great damage or ruin.

enslaved (en-SLAYVD) Made someone be a slave.

herald (HER-uld) An official messenger or a person who carries important news or royal proclamations.

humiliating (hyoo-MIH-lee-ayt-ing) Making someone else feel very bad about himself or herself.

immortal (ih-MOR-tul) Never able to die.

immortality (ih-mor-TAH-lih-tee) The ability to live forever.

intervene (in-ter-VEEN) To interfere in someone else's affairs.

missions (MIH-shunz) Special jobs or tasks.

mortal (MOR-tul) A human being or a living creature.

mythology (mih-THAH-lah-jee) A body of stories that people make up to explain events.

offends (uh-FENDZ) Causes someone to feel angry, upset, or hurt due to something that was said or done.

oracle (AWR-uh-kul) A person who was able to know things that have not happened yet. In Greek mythology, the gods were said to speak through an oracle.

pelt (PELT) An animal skin with the fur still on it.

penance (PEH-nunts) An action a person has to do in order to show that he or she is sorry or sad about something he or she has done that was wrong.

sentinels (SENT-ih-nelz) Guards or people, often soldiers, who watch over something.

tedious (TEE-dee-us) Long, slow, and boring.

trenches (TRENCH-ez) Long, narrow ditches dug in the ground.

underworld (UN-dur-wurld) The place where the souls of the dead live.

victorious (vik-TOR-ee-us) Having won something, such as a battle or a race.

Index

Websites

Due to the changing nature of Internet links, PowerKids Press has developed an online list of websites related to the subject of this book. This site is updated regularly. Please use this link to access the list:

www.powerkidslinks.com/grmy/labors